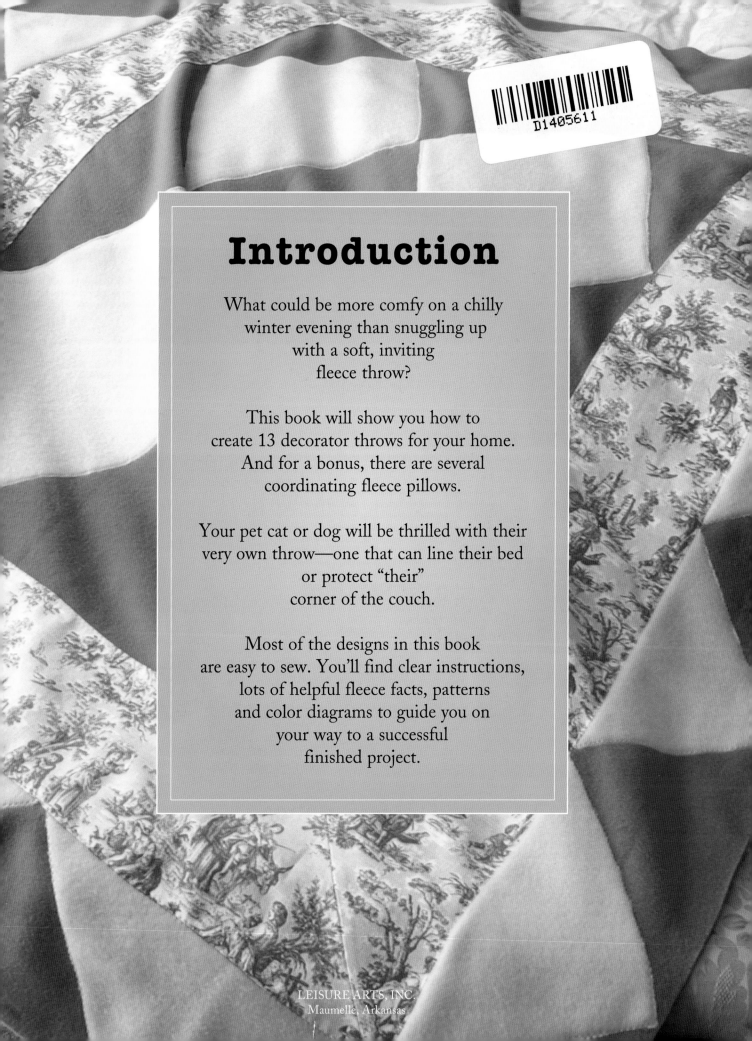

Introduction

What could be more comfy on a chilly
winter evening than snuggling up
with a soft, inviting
fleece throw?

This book will show you how to
create 13 decorator throws for your home.
And for a bonus, there are several
coordinating fleece pillows.

Your pet cat or dog will be thrilled with their
very own throw—one that can line their bed
or protect "their"
corner of the couch.

Most of the designs in this book
are easy to sew. You'll find clear instructions,
lots of helpful fleece facts, patterns
and color diagrams to guide you on
your way to a successful
finished project.

LEISURE ARTS, INC.
Maumelle, Arkansas

Table of

2

Contents

Fleece Facts

The following are a few facts, tips and instructions to help make it even easier to work with this wonderfully soft, easy-to-sew fabric:

1. We used fleece that was 60" wide for all the projects in this book. Cut off the selvage edges before measuring the fleece.

2. It's important when using fleece to determine the right and wrong side. To find the right side of the fleece, stretch the fabric along the cut edge. The fleece will curl to the wrong side. When you determine the right side of the fleece, be sure to mark all your cut pieces before you start sewing, either with a small piece of tape or lightly with a marking pencil.

3. Length of stitch to use: Because fleece stretches and waves, it's important to use a loose stitch. We recommend using 9 stitches per inch. If you're stitching through more than two layers, increase the stitch length. The length depends on the amount of layers. Experiment with your machine .

4. Pressure: If you're having trouble with the fleece feeding through your machine, try lessening the pressure on the presser foot.

5. Sewing machine needles: Use a universal or ball point needle. Check the package of needles that adapt to your machine for fabric weight suggestions.

6. Embellishing: When you're applying appliques or adding trims, you can either use pins or a double-sided tape. A dab of fabric glue works well when adding cording.

7. Transferring the patterns: To make a pattern, trace each piece separately onto tracing paper, then trace the pattern onto a piece of heavy paper such as cardstock. Cut out pattern. To cut fleece piece, draw around pattern using a Chacopel pencil before cutting out, or pin tracing paper pattern to fleece and cut out the piece even with the edge of the pattern.

8. Fabric care: Fleece doesn't shrink and is colorfast. There's no need for pre-washing.

For laundering, use a powdered laundry detergent and luke warm water. Be sure the machine is set on the gentle cycle and set for low heat. Liquid fabric softeners and sheets should not be used.

For ironing, use steam and a pressing cloth. Never touch the iron to the fleece directly.

9. Hemming edges or lining fleece is optional. This depends on your own personal preference.

General supplies
Scissors or rotary cutter
Measuring tape
Yard stick
Fabric marker
Pins
Fabric glue
Needle
Marking pens
Tracing paper and cardstock

Fleece:
1¾ yd. blue
1¾ yd. yellow
Also:
1¼ yd. blue-and-yellow
 toile fabric
Yellow thread

A Day in the Country

1. Cut the blue fleece 60" x 48".

2. Use the patterns on pages 40 and 41 to cut four diamonds and 14 triangles of yellow fleece.

3. Cut four strips of toile fabric, two, 49" x 7" and two, 37" x 7."

4. Turn the long sides of each strip under ½" and press.

5. Form a rectangle by sewing the strips together, mitering the corners. Make sure measurements and stitching of mitered corners are precise to ensure a perfect rectangle.

6. Position the rectangle and triangles on the fleece as shown in diagram below. Tuck ¼" of the base of each triangle under the strip of the toile fabric.

7. Pin in place and use a zigzag stitch around the inside and outside edges of the toile and sides of the triangles.

8. Position the diamond shapes in the center of the rectangle as shown and pin in place. Use a zigzag stitch around the edges of the diamonds.

Hint

When using a zigzag stitch on the inside corners, continue $^1/_8$" beyond the corner, ending with the needle down on the fabric being appliqued. Raise the pressure foot and turn the fabric, lower the pressure foot and continue stitching.

When you're using a print fabric such as the toile design in this project, be sure to cut the fabric with the design or motif in the appropriate direction.

Inspired by French country design, this lovely toile-trimmed throw beautifully accents the lush bedroom décor. Diamonds of butter yellow and French blue adorn the center, while triangles border the outside. All of the pieces of this throw are top stitched, not pieced, so the construction is simple. The finished throw, simply lovely.

Trimmed with hand-cut fringe, this heavenly throw is perfect for the person who enjoys a cool evening on the front porch. Stars and stripes in shades of fuchsia, turquoise and purple gracefully adorn this classic black throw. Sit yourself in a comfy rocker snuggled into this cloud from heaven and look to the skies.

Star Gazer

. Cut both black and turquoise fleece
 measure 56" long and 43" wide.

. Using the pattern on page 45, cut
ut two stars each of pink, turquoise
nd purple.

. Cut two strips each 43" long of pink,
urple, and turquoise.

. On the right side of the black fleece,
easure in 14" from the top and
ottom edge. Place the first strip of
rim and pin or glue in place. Measure
 ¾" from the first strip and position
he second strip and pin. Repeat for
he third strip measuring in from the
econd (see diagram). Use a zigzag
titch along the edges of the trim.

5. Position and pin the stars on the
throw as pictured. Stitch around each
star using a zigzag stitch.

6. With right sides together, pin the
sides of black and turquoise fleece
together and sew up the two sides with
a ½" seam allowance.

7. To form the fringe: Turn the throw
right side out and lay it flat on a
cutting table. At each end, cut through
both black and turquoise fleece to
make fringe. Cut each strip of fringe
½" wide and 4" long. Tie one black
strip and one turquoise strip of fringe
together. Continue doing this across
the throw.

Fleece:
1¾ yds. black
1¾ yds. turquoise
⅓ yd. pink,
⅓ yd. purple
Also:
Fleece strips -
¾ wide: 2½ yds. each pink,
  turquoise, purple
Black thread
Fabric glue

Hint

Many fabric stores sell
fleece strips. If you are
unable to find this pre-cut
trim, allow for extra fabric
to make your own.

To mark the fleece before
cutting fringe, measure up
4" on each side of fleece
and mark with a pencil.
Lay a yard stick from mark
to mark and draw a line.
Continue across marking
every ½". Cut from edge
to line every ½" across the
throw.

Fleece:
2 yds. red
1¼ yds. red-and-black
   check
¾ yd. black
Also:
2½ yds. of 2"w black
   fringe
Black thread

Hint

The fringe for this throw could also be made using the checked fleece and hand cutting it (see page 23, step 5 for instructions on hand cutting the fringe). For a different look, use black fleece squares in each corner of the throw. Sew a large button covered with the black-and-red checked fabric in the center of the middle square.

Welcome to the Lodge

1. Cut red fleece 44" x 50". Cut red-and-black check fleece 30" x 30".

2. Cut four pieces of red-and-black check fleece 10" x 7".

3. For triangles, cut one each 15½" square of red and black solid fleece. Then cut diagonally across the squares.

4. Using a ½" seam allowance, stitch the sides of the triangles together following the diagram. Pin this to the red-and-black checked fleece squares as shown in the diagram below. Use a zigzag stitch to sew around the edges.

5. Center the triangles and the check square on the red fleece. Pin in place. Stitch around the edges of the check fleece using a zigzag stitch.

6. Place the remaining four pieces on the throw, one in each corner. Pin in place and stitch around the edges using a zigzag stitch.

7. Cut the fringe to fit two sides of the throw and sew in place using a zigzag stitch.

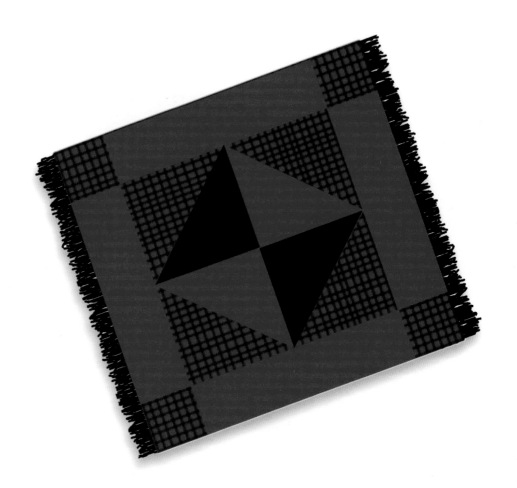

Come on in and make yourself at home. Snuggle into this patchwork throw and dream about fishing in the nearby lake. Blocks of red and black are artfully patched together with fringe added to each end, for a soft, cozy throw just right for a rustic cabin.

This folk art–inspired throw and pillow will fit right into a country home, whether it's rustic, traditional or cottage style. Each patchwork square is layered with blanket stitched circles in country colors and displayed on a field of black. The coordinating pillow adds a touch of class to this homey setting.

Folk Art "Quilt"

Throw

1. Cut black fleece 55" x 40".

2. Cut 10" squares: two each of green, lavender and burgundy.

3. Using the patterns on pages 42 and 43 cut out the circles and squares.

4. Following the diagram, assemble the quilt squares by sewing large and small circles onto the 10" squares using a blanket stitch and four strands of black embroidery floss.

5. Position the squares on the black fleece 8½" from sides and 7" from each end with 4½" between squares. Follow the diagram for placement. Pin in place.

6. Sew on the squares using a zigzag stitch and black thread.

Pillow

1. Cut two 19" black squares.

2. Using the patterns on pages 42 and 43 cut out the circles and squares

3. Follow the diagram to assemble the pieces. Sew the large and small circles onto the squares using a blanket stitch and four strands of black embroidery floss (see "blanket stitching" at right).

4. Position the squares on the black pillow piece and pin. Sew in place using a zigzag stitch and black thread.

5. With right sides together, sew the black squares together on three sides using ½" seam allowance.

6. Clip seams, turn the pillow right side out, and insert the pillow form. Turn the edges of the opening under ½" and hand sew together.

Supplies

Throw
Fleece:
1¾ yd. black
½ yd. each green, lavender, burgundy
¼ yd. camel
Also:
Black thread
Black embroidery floss
#24 chenille needle

Pillow
Fleece:
¾ yd. black
¼ yd. each green, lavender, burgundy and camel
Also:
18" pillow form
Black thread
Black embroidery floss
#24 chenille needle

Hint

Blanket stitch instructions:
1. Come up at 1. Go down at 2 and come up at 3, keeping floss below point of needle.

Continue stitching, keeping stitches even.

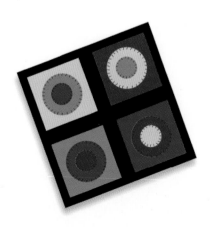

Supplies

Throw
Fleece:
2 yds. blue
½ yd. each of red and white
Also:
White embroidery floss
White thread
#24 chenille needle

Pillow
Fleece:
¼ yd. each red and white
¾ yd. blue
Also:
18" pillow form
Blue thread
White embroidery floss
#24 chenille needle

Hint

To make this a quicker project, you can elect to machine-sew instead of blanket stitch the star to the throw and pillow. Use white thread and a zigzag stitch.

If you'd like to add embellishments, sew white tassels to each corner of the throw and pillow.

Throw

1. Cut blue fleece 60" x 44".

2. Cut strips of fleece as follows: one white and one red, 8½" x 24", one white and one red, 9" x 24".

3. Cut out a star from the blue fleece using the pattern on page 45.

4. To make the center section of the throw: Sew the 9" wide red and white strips together using a ½" seam allowance.

5. Again, using a ½ seam allowance, sew the 8½" red and white strips to the 9" strips as shown in the diagram.

6. Position the star on the strips and pin. Use a blanket stitch (see "blanket stitching" page 13) around the edge of the star, using four strands of the embroidery floss.

7. Place the center section that you've just created on the large piece of blue fleece (refer to diagram for placement). Pin in place and zigzag stitch around all four sides with white thread.

Pillow

1. Cut a square of blue fleece 19" x 19".

2. Use the smaller star pattern on page 45. Cut the star from blue fleece.

3. Cut two strips of red fleece and one of white fleece, each 7" x 19".

4. Sew the strips together with the white strip in the center using ½" seam allowances. This forms the front of the pillow.

5. Position the star on the front (see diagram) and pin in place. Use four strands of embroidery floss to blanket stitch around the edges (see "blanket stitching" page 13).

6. With right sides together, sew blue back piece to the pillow front on three sides using ½" seam allowance.

7. Clip corners, turn the pillow right side out, and insert the pillow form. Turn the edges of the opening under ½" and hand sew closed.

Wrap yourself in Americana—three cheers for the red, white and blue. A bright five point star on brilliant stripes of red and white adorns a solid field of blue. Combined with a matching pillow and embellished with blanket stitching, this patriotic pair will surely get you in the spirit.

Cultivate a garden of blossoms to decorate this enchanting throw. Life-like petals in cool shades of turquoise and purple grow on a ground of misty green all fenced in with the matching strips of fleece trim. This fun and fancy creation is ideal for chilly spring evenings or crisp summer mornings at the beach cottage.

Forever in Bloom

. Cut light green fleece to measure
4" long and 38" wide.

. Cut fleece strips as follows: purple,
ne 54" long, one 38" long; turquoise,
ne strip 54" long and one 38" long.

. Using the pattern on page 46 and
7, cut out flowers: 2 each of purple
nd turquoise. Cut out circles for
enter of the flowers; two each of
urple and turquoise. Cut out 15 dark
reen leaves.

. Position the trim on the throw
" from the edge. See diagram for
lacement. Pin or use dots of fabric
lue to secure in place.

. Use a zigzag stitch to sew the edges
f the trim to the throw. Note: use
oordinating thread for trim, center
f flowers, leaves and cord.

6. Place flowers and flower centers on
throw (see photo or diagram) and pin.
Zigzag stitch around edges of flower
centers. Let petals remain loose.

7. Position leaves on throw referring
to diagram and pin in place. Use zigzag
stitch around edges of leaves.

8. Lay cording on throw referring to
diagram. Use dots of fabric glue to
hold in place. Use a zigzag stitch over
the top of the cord.

Fleece:
1⅓ yds. light green
⅓ yd. turquoise
⅓ yd. purple
⅛ yd. dark green
Also:
Fleece strips, 2¾ yd. each
  purple and turquoise
1¼ yd. dark green cord
Purple, turquoise, dark
  green thread
Fabric glue

Hint

If you don't like the idea of
the petals being loose, use
a zigzag stitch all around
the outside edge of the
blossoms. Use alternate
colors of the thread for an
interesting look; turquoise
on purple and vice versa.
The petals could also
be blanket stitched for a
more folk art look. See
page 13 for blanket stitch
instructions.
Another finishing idea for
this throw is to round the
corners.

Fleece:
1½ yds. royal blue
⅓ yd. purple
⅓ yd. lavender
⅓ yd. variegated pink
Also:
12 – 1½" buttons to cover
Blue thread

Buttons & Patches

1. Cut royal blue fleece to measure 52" long and 40" wide.

2. Cut four 8" x 8" squares each of purple, lavender and pink fleece.

3. Position and pin squares on the blue fleece, 4" apart, starting 4" in from each edge. See photo or the diagram below.

4. Use a zigzag stitch and blue thread to sew the squares to the blue fleece.

5. Using a straight stitch, divide each square into four sections by sewing down the center horizontally and vertically.

6. Cover buttons with alternating colors of fleece (following manufacturer's instructions). Sew the buttons to the throw as pictured.

Hint

As an alternative to covered buttons, make fleece tassels to sew to squares.

To make a fleece tassel: Cut six strips of fleece ½" x 8". Place four strips together and tie in the middle with one of the strips. Fold the strips in half and knot them with the sixth strip. Try making the tassels with all three colors of the fleece for a fun, multicolored look.

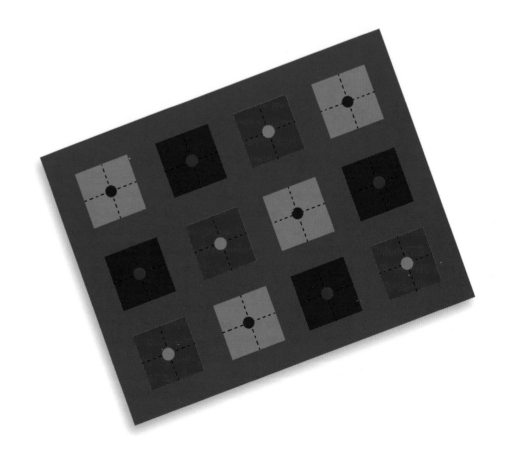

Puffed up squares of cheerful colors grace this stylish throw. Each square is accented in the center with a jumbo covered button in a contrasting shade of purple, pink or lavender. Drape this throw over a chair or the end of your bed and it's ready to perform as a foot warmer, par excellence.

19

Become an armchair traveler visiting exotic locales covered up in your paisley emblazoned throw. Images of Kashmir or Casablanca will dance in your dreams when you nap under this exotic afghan. The throw and matching pillow are studded with shiny beads and edged with a beaded trim. Bon Voyage!

20

Pretty Paisley

Throw

1. Cut the black fleece 60" x 44" and two strips of red fleece 8" x 44".

2. Cut out paisley pieces using patterns on page 48.

3. Assemble the paisley pieces as in the diagram and sew together using a zigzag stitch and matching threads. Sew them on the red strips using a zigzag stitch (refer to diagram).

4. Place the cord on the red strips and glue in a few places. Sew over the green cording using a zigzag stitch.

5. Hand sew the loose beads on the paisley pieces (refer to photo).

6. Position the red strips on the black fleece 6" from the top and bottom edge. Use a zigzag stitch and red thread to sew all around the four sides.

7. Sew the beaded trim on the top and bottom edges of the throw.

Pillow

1. Cut two pieces of red fleece 19"x19".

2. Cut out paisley pieces using patterns on page 48. Stitch the paisley pieces together as in the diagram using a zigzag stitch.

3. Using corresponding thread colors and a zigzag stitch, sew the paisley pieces to red pillow front.

4. Position the green cording on the pillow front. Glue in spots, then use a zigzag stitch to sew over the cord.

5. Hand sew the beads on the paisley pieces.

6. Lay the pillow front right side up. Align raw edges of pillow and beaded trim together with beads toward the center and pin. Machine stitch in place as close as possible to beads.

7. To finish, follow the pillow instructions on page 13, steps 5 and 6.

Supplies

Throw
Fleece:
2 yds. black
½ yd. red
¼ yd. purple
⅛ yd. royal blue
Also:
2½ yds. beaded trim
Small beads: 6 ea gold, pink, blue and green
2 yds. green cord, ⅛" wide
Thread: green, red, purple, turquoise and blue

Pillow
Fleece:
¾ yd. red
⅛ yd. each of purple, turquoise, and royal blue
Also:
18" pillow form
1 yd. green cord, ⅛" wide
Small beads – 3 ea. pink, gold and green
2 yds. beaded fringe
Thread: red, purple, turquoise and blue

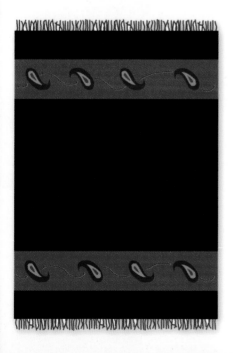

Hint

Lay bead trim on a strip of masking tape to hold in place while stitching to fleece. Use a zipper foot to sew on the beaded trim.

Fleece:
2 yds. variegated pink
1 yd. Southwest style print
Also:
Pink thread

Native Woods

1. Cut variegated fleece to measure 60" long and 44" wide.

2. Cut two strips of printed fleece 44" long and 8" wide. Cut two more strips of printed fleece 44" long and 3" wide for the fringe.

3. Position one 8" wide strip across the width of the throw, in 10" from top edge (see diagram). Repeat with the second strip at the opposite end. (Note: right side of throw and right side of strips should be facing up.)

4. Pin strips in place and use a zigzag stitch to sew along the horizontal edges.

Hint

There's a vast array of printed fleece available at your local fabric store. Combining a print with a solid fleece is a fun challenge when you're making your fabric choice. Be sure to take a sample of your furniture fabric or a paint swatch with you to the fabric store so that you can coordinate the fleece colors to your own decor.

Take comfort next to the fire and enjoy the winter season wrapped in this richly colored throw. Reminiscent of Native American design, the colorful strips and fringe add a touch of drama. The suede-like background is a subtle tie-dyed fleece which coordinates nicely with the vivid print.

. Make the fringe by making 2¼"
ong cuts ½" apart across the 3" wide
rinted fleece (see diagram). To add
he fringe: with right side of throw
nd right side of strip facing up,
osition the 3" wide strip ½" under
he top edge of the throw. Sew along
he edge of the throw with a straight
titch. Repeat at the opposite end.

When the temperature dips and it's time to come inside for warmth, invite yourself in to sit down next to a cozy fire. Settle in under this plush snowflake-covered throw and sip your hot chocolate while listening to the crackling fire. Embellished with snowflake appliques and edged with a whimsical ball fringe, this blue and white throw is the perfect accessory for a mountain cabin.

Home is Where the Hearth Is

Measure and cut snowflake fabric [ ]" long and 40" wide.

Using the pattern on page 38, cut [ ]t four snowflakes.

Cut out four pieces of white fleece [m]easuring 12" x 14" each.

Center the snowflakes on white [fl]eece as shown in diagram and pin [i]n place. Use a straight stitch to sew [d]own the center of each "spoke" of the [s]nowflake. Note: Stitch down the ends [o]f the snowflake if you want them to [l]y flat.

5. Position white pieces on the snowflake print fleece as shown, and using a zigzag stitch, stitch in place.

6. Sew ball fringe along top and bottom edges of throw.

Supplies

Fleece:
2 yds. snowflake print
½ yd. white
Also:
2½ yds. white ball fringe, 1¾" wide
Blue and white thread

Hint

We used a ball fringe to trim this throw, but you might try an alternate trim such as a white cotton knot fringe or a tassel trim. Your local fabric store has a huge selection of trims to choose from.
You could also hand cut the fringe by cutting strips on each edge of the throw 4" in length by ½" wide. If you decide to do this, you'll have to add 8" to the length of your throw.
If you have leftover fleece, make a matching pillow that has just one white square and snowflake. Edge the pillow with ball fringe. Or make the pillow and snowflake with the white fleece and the print for the square.

Fleece:
2½ yds. camel
½ yd. green
Also:
5 yds. green cord, ⅛" wide
2½ yds. green bullion
   fringe, 3" wide
Green and camel thread
Fabric glue

Hint

Experiment with your own vine and leaf design. When you're happy with the results, hold the leaves in place with pins and the vines with fabric glue.

You might wish to back this throw with the green fleece and hand cut the fringe as we did in the Star Gazer Throw on page 9. To do this you'll need to add 8" to the length of your throw.

Autumn Leaves

1. Cut camel colored fleece 44" wide and 60" long.

2. Cut a second piece of camel fleece 12½" wide and 30" long.

3. Cut the green fleece 12½" wide and 30" long.

4. Use the pattern on page 45 to cut 6 camel leaves and 6 green leaves.

5. To form the inset for the throw: use a straight stitch to sew the small pieces of green and camel fleece together on one long edge using a ½" seam allowance.

6. Mark and position the leaves and cording on the insets. Pin leaves to hold in place and use small dots of fabric glue to hold cording in place.

Stitch around the leaves and over the cording using a zigzag stitch. Again, use thread to match fleece.

7. Position the wrong side of the inset on the right side of the large camel piece as shown in the diagram. Pin in place, then use a zigzag stitch to sew this piece in place. Use green thread on green piece and camel thread on camel piece.

8. Measure out 1" from the inset for cording border. Secure in place with small dots of fabric glue, then stitch over the cord using a zigzag stitch.

9. Sew the fringe along each end of the throw.

This leaf–scattered throw is infused with the luscious colors of nature. The handsome camel background fits in with any neutral décor. An unusual reflective design cleverly showcases the vining and climbing leaves in all their splendor. The finishing touch—a thick twisted fringe gracing each end of the throw.

Settle in with a good book, a glass of wine and this warm and fuzzy afghan. Adorned with stylized berries and leaves, this throw will have you feeling so pampered and spoiled you'll never want to venture outside. The berries are yo-yos made of fleece and sewn on for dimensional interest, the vine, a simple braided trim. How sweet it is!

Sweeter Than Wine

. Cut burgundy fleece 60" x 44", the
amel fleece, 39" x 24".

. Using the pattern on page 45, cut
ut 18 green leaves and 14 lavender
ircles (for the berries).

. Position and pin the camel fleece
n the center of the burgundy piece
ollowing the diagram. With a zigzag
titch and camel thread, sew around
he edges of the camel fleece.

. To make the berries: Use the
avender circles you've cut previously.
Hand sew a running stitch around the
ircles ¼" from the edge. Place a small
mount of fiberfill in the center of the

circle. Pull the thread gently to gather
the fabric around the fiberfill. Tie the
ends of the thread together to secure.

5. Follow the diagram for the
placement of the leaves and cord. Pin
leaves in place and sew using green
thread and a zigzag stitch. Glue
cording in spots and stitch over the
cord using a zigzag stitch.

6. Hand stitch the berries following
the diagram.

Supplies

Fleece:
1¾ yd. burgundy
1¼ yd. camel
¼ yd. green
¼ yd. lavender
Also:
5 yds. green cord, ⅛" wide
Green, camel and lavender
  thread
Polyester fiberfill
Needle

Hint

To give extra stability to
the berries when stitching
them on, hand-stitch both
horizontally and vertically
on the back of the berry.
As an alternative to making
the berries, you might use
large pom poms instead.
Large buttons would also
work nicely.

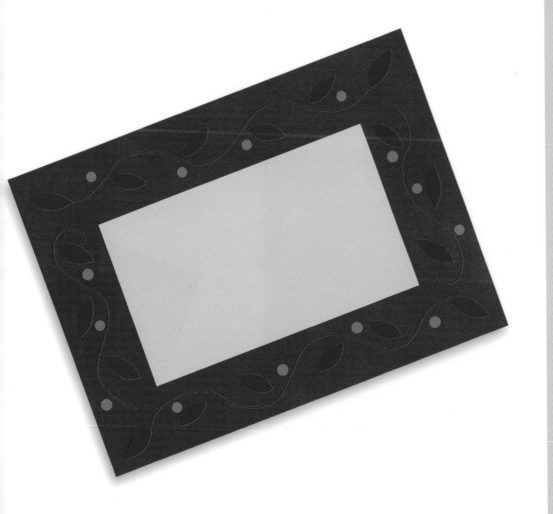

Supplies

Throw
Fleece:
1¼ yd. tartan plaid
1 yd. dark green
1 yd. dark blue (This will
be enough fabric for the
throw and pillow. If you
make the pillow only, see
below.)
Also:
Dark blue thread

Pillow
Fleece:
¾ yd. tartan plaid
½ yd. dark green
½ yd. dark blue
Also:
Dark blue thread
18" pillow form
Needle

Hint

To speed up this project, you can cut several same-size squares at one time. We used a straight stitch for sewing on the squares, but you might want to vary the look of this throw by using a zigzag stitch. For a more folk art look, you can sew the squares on using a blanket stitch. For blanket stitch instructions see page 13.

Throw

1. Cut out a 19" square pattern.

2. Place the pattern on the fabric and cut out six squares of tartan plaid, 3 each of dark green and dark blue.

3. Use a ½" seam allowance to stitch the squares together following the diagram below for placement.

4. To hem the throw, turn the fleece under ½" on all four sides and stitch.

Pillow

1. Draw and cut out patterns of 19", 9", 6" and 3" squares.

2. Position the square patterns on the fabric and cut out the following: tartan plaid - one 19" square, four 3" squares; blue – two 9" squares, two 6" squares; green – two 9" squares, two 6" squares.

3. Center the 3" tartan squares on the 6" green and blue squares and top stitch around edges.

4. Center the 6" green squares on the 9" blue squares and the 6" blue squares on the 9" green squares. Top stitch around edges.

5. Following the diagram, stitch 9" squares together using a ½" seam allowance to make the front of the pillow.

6. Using a ½" seam allowance and with right sides together, stitch large tartan square and pillow front together leaving one side open.

7. Clip seams, then turn pillow right side out. Insert pillow form, turn edges of opening under ½" and hand stitch closed.

Oh the weather outside is frightful but the inside is so inviting. Especially when you're as snug as a bug in this soft and cuddly throw. Pieced together with squares of solid blue, forest green and a coordinating tartan plaid, this coverlet is just the thing for keeping toasty warm on a cold winter's evening. A matching pillow adds to this comfortable setting and gives you an extra reason to relax.

A rustic lodge in the woods or a masculine retreat would both be ideal settings for this pair of pillows straight from the northwoods. Chenille fringe trims the edges of the pillows, each one embellished with scenic patches representing nature and the outdoors.

Cabin Fever

Tree Pillow

. Cut two 15" squares of brown fleece.

. Cut camel fleece 9" x 11".

. Cut four pieces of the print fleece ¼" long and 3¼" wide each.

. Position the tree fleece pieces on the camel piece as shown in the diagram. Pin in place and zigzag stitch around all the edges using camel thread.

. Place the camel piece on one brown square (see diagram) and pin in place. Zigzag stitch around the edges of the camel piece with camel thread.

. With raw edges aligned, and the fringe toward the center, pin fringe to the pillow top with right sides together. Stitch fringe in place.

. Using a ½" seam allowance and right sides together, sew the brown squares together on three sides following the fringe stitch line.

. Clip the corners and turn right side out. Insert the pillow form. Turn the edges of the opening under ½" and hand sew closed.

Deer Pillow

1. Cut two 15" squares of navy blue fleece.

2. Cut camel fleece to measure 9" x 11".

3. Cut deer fleece pieces to measure 5½" x 5½" and the flower piece, 2½" x 5½".

4. Follow steps 4 through 9 of the Cabin Fever Tree pillow to complete this pillow.

Tree Pillow

Deer Pillow

Supplies

Pillow with tree design
Fleece:
½ yd. brown
½ yd. camel
¼ yd. northwoods print
Also:
14" pillow form
1¾ yd. brown chenille fringe
Camel and brown thread

Pillow with deer design
Fleece:
½ yd. each navy blue and camel
¼ yd. northwoods print
Also:
1¾ yd. brown chenille fringe
Camel and navy blue thread

Hint

If you can't find the exact print used here, there are many others to choose from. Cut the print that you've chosen following the design of the print and fit it to your pillow front.

Fleece:
1 yd. lavender
Also:
½ yd. pink checked fabric
Double sided fusible
  webbing
Black thread

Hint

To make the kitty appliques
more secure, use a zigzag
stitch around each one.

To embellish the kitty
cut-outs, sew a tiny bow
at each neck. Sew or glue
tiny buttons for the kitty's
eyes.

Buttons could also be
spaced and sewn across
the checked border.

Basketful of Love

1. Cut fleece 40" x 30". Cut two strips
of the checked fabric 2½" x 30½".

2. Turn all four edges of the pink
checked fabric under ¼" and press
with iron.

3. Position the strips on the fleece
(see diagram) and pin. Use a zigzag
stitch and black thread to sew around
the edges.

4. Cut a piece of checked fabric and
a piece of fusible webbing 3" x 10".

Follow manufacturer's instructions to fuse the fabric. Trace the cat pattern on page 48 onto the webbing and cut out.

5. Position the cut-out cats on the fleece and fuse using the iron and a pressing cloth (don't touch iron directly to fleece).

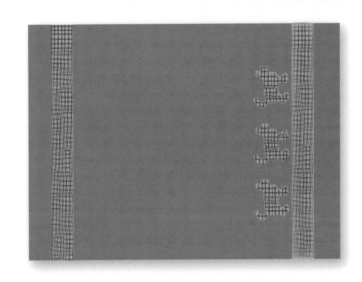

Cat tested by Abbie, this throw has received the feline seal of approval. A lovely shade of lavender is the backdrop for the pink appliqued kitties marching single file along the border. Tucked into a basket, this soft, fluffy blanket is sure to delight your favorite pet.

Your pooch will love you unconditionally when you add this nice fluffy throw to his bed. Trimmed with strips of snappy gingham fabric and an orderly parade of pups, this fleece coverlet is sure to become his favorite possession. And it will be yours too, when it's protecting your favorite piece of furniture.

Puppy Love

1. Cut fleece 40" x 30". Cut two strips of the black-and-white checked fabric 1½" x 30½".

2. Turn all four edges of checked fabric under ¼" and press with iron.

3. Position the strips on the fleece (see diagram below) and pin. Zigzag stitch around the edges using black thread.

4. Cut a piece of checked fabric and a piece of fusible webbing 3" x 10". Follow manufacturer's instructions to fuse the fabric. Trace the dog pattern on page 48 onto the webbing and cut out.

5. Position the cut-out dogs on the fleece and fuse using the iron and a pressing cloth (don't touch iron directly to fleece).

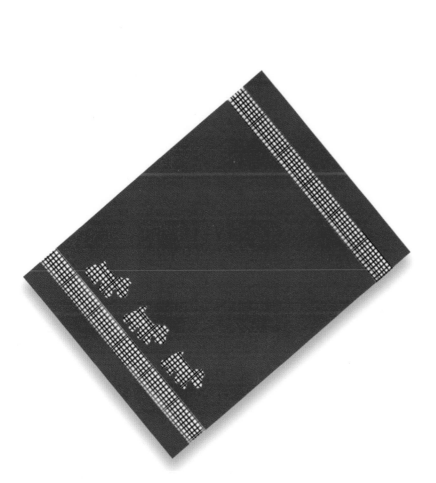

Supplies

Fleece:
1 yd. red
Also:
½ yd. black & white
  checked fabric
Double sided fusible
  webbing
Black thread

Hint

These throws are so easy and quick, you might want to make several for all your dog-loving friends. You can vary the color of the fleece and checked fabric to suit the taste of each recipient.

Why not tuck the throw into a basket and add some doggie treats, a new leash, and other pet pleasing gift items? Wrap the basket in cellophane and add a big bow tied up with some dog bones.

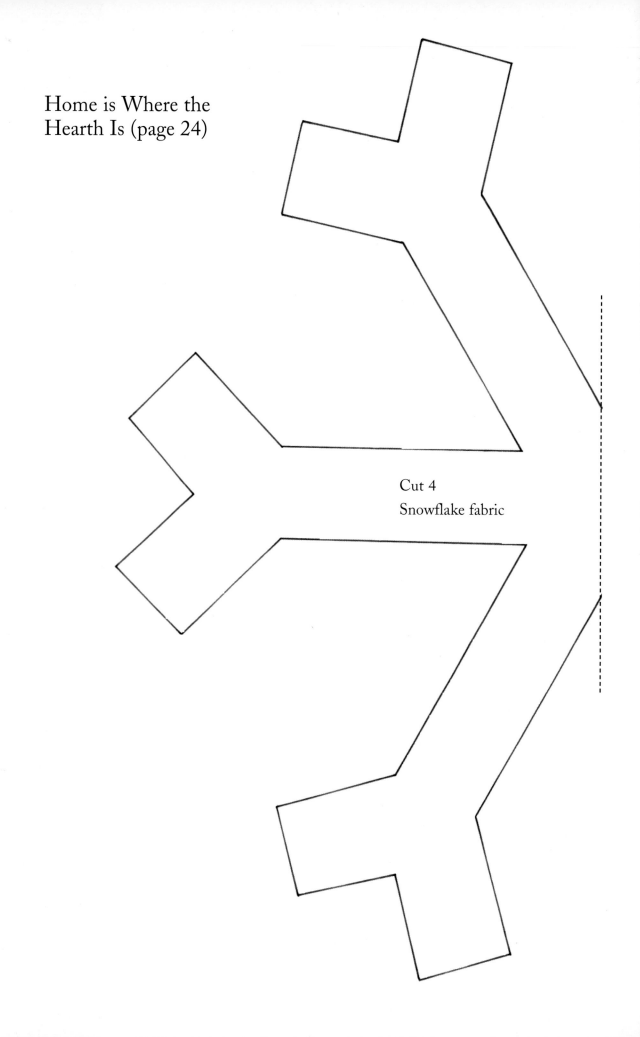

Cut 4

Snowflake fabric

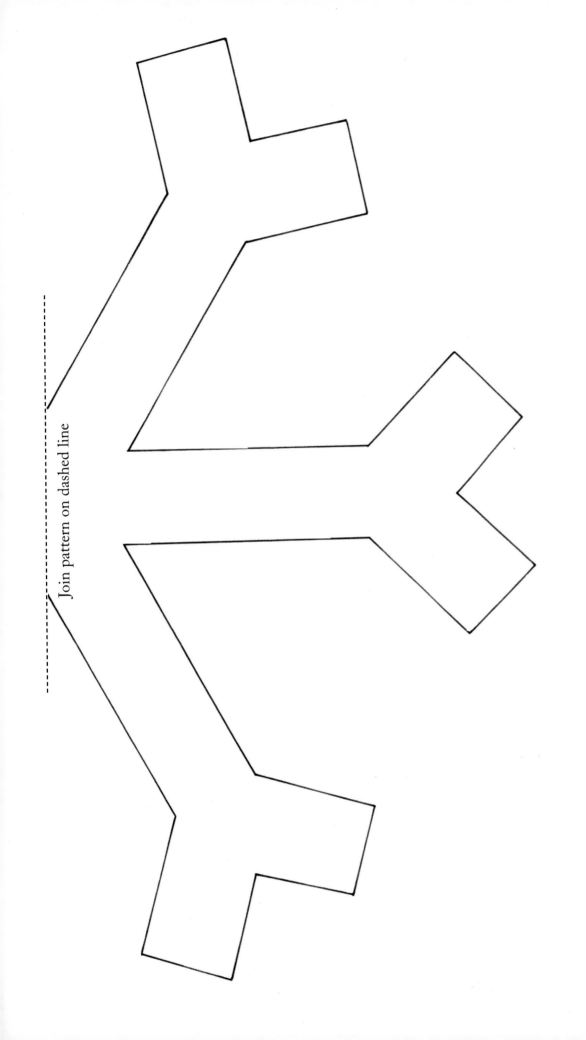

Join pattern on dashed line

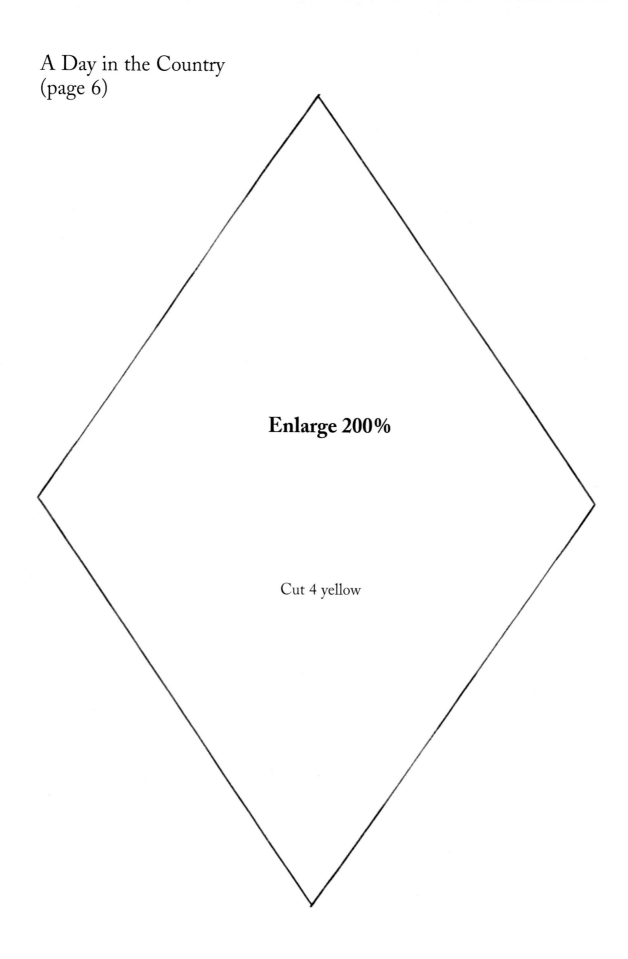

Enlarge 200%

Cut 4 yellow

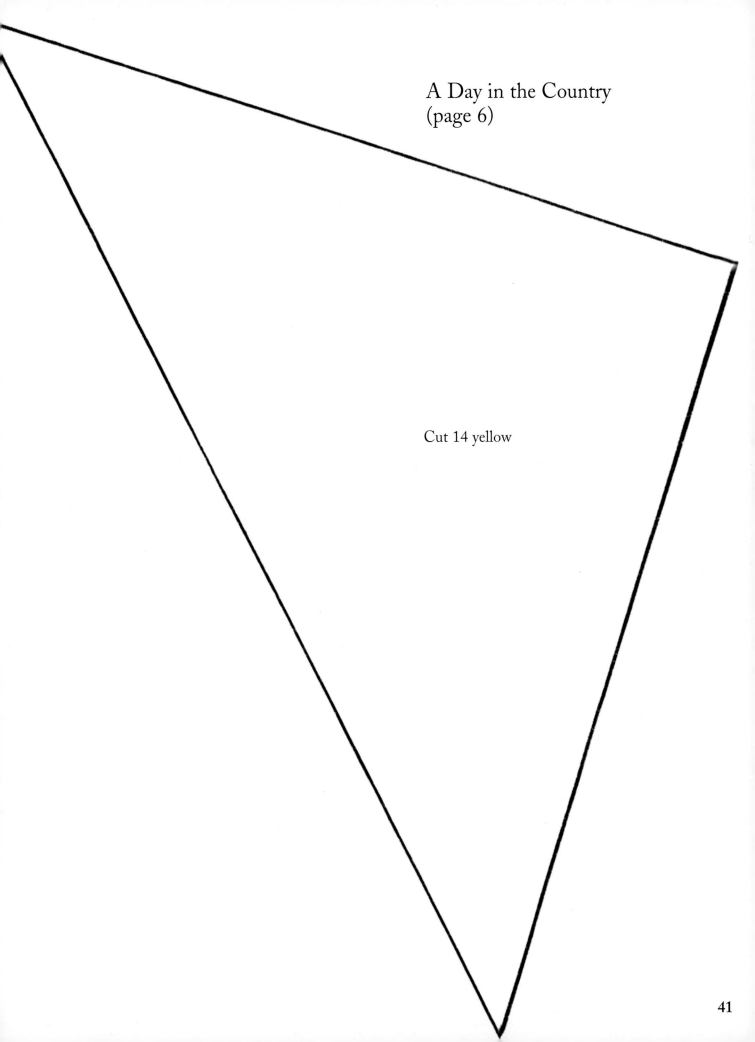

A Day in the Country
(page 6)

Cut 14 yellow

Folk Art "Quilt"
(page 11)

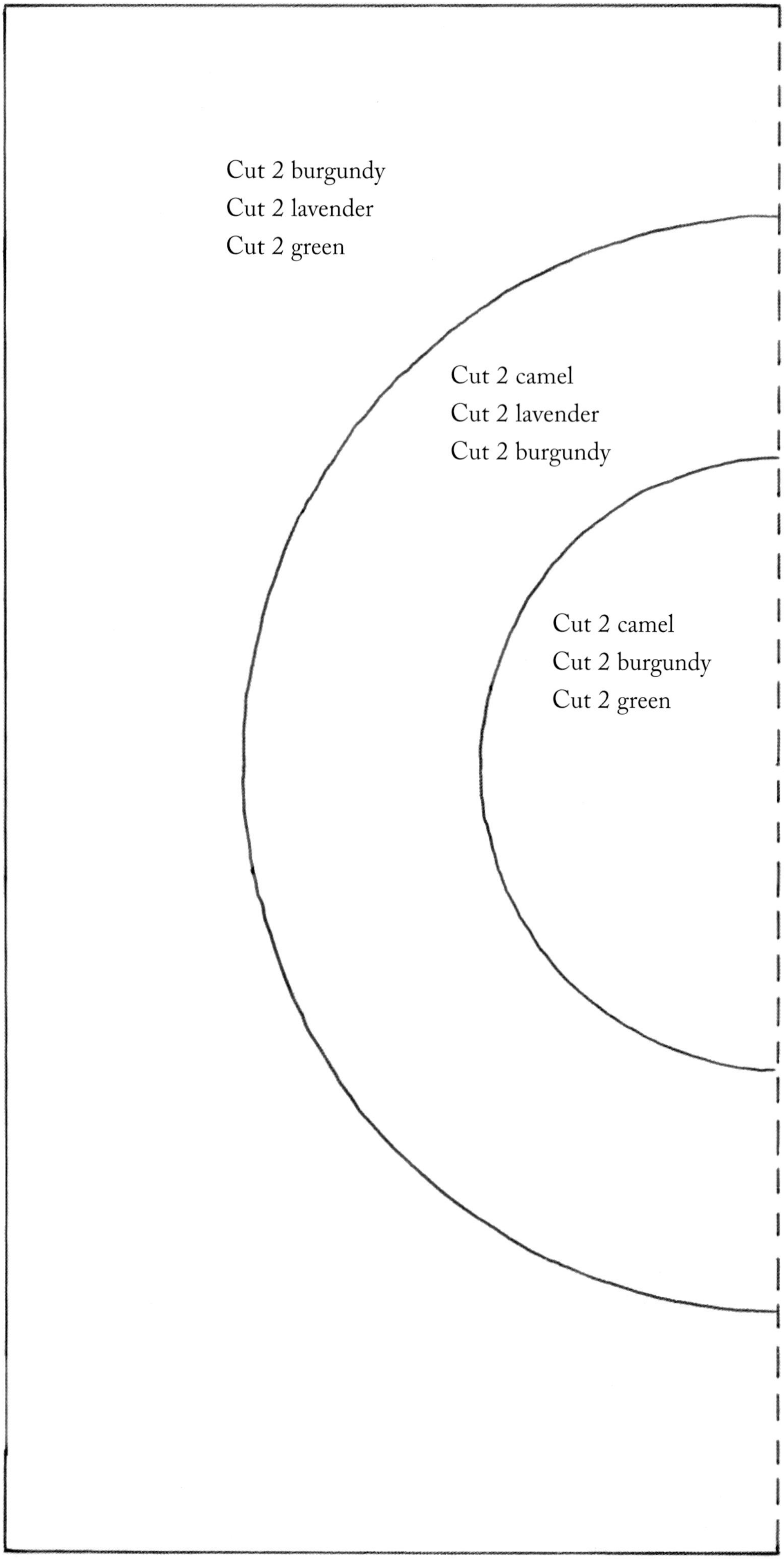

Cut 2 burgundy
Cut 2 lavender
Cut 2 green

Cut 2 camel
Cut 2 lavender
Cut 2 burgundy

Cut 2 camel
Cut 2 burgundy
Cut 2 green

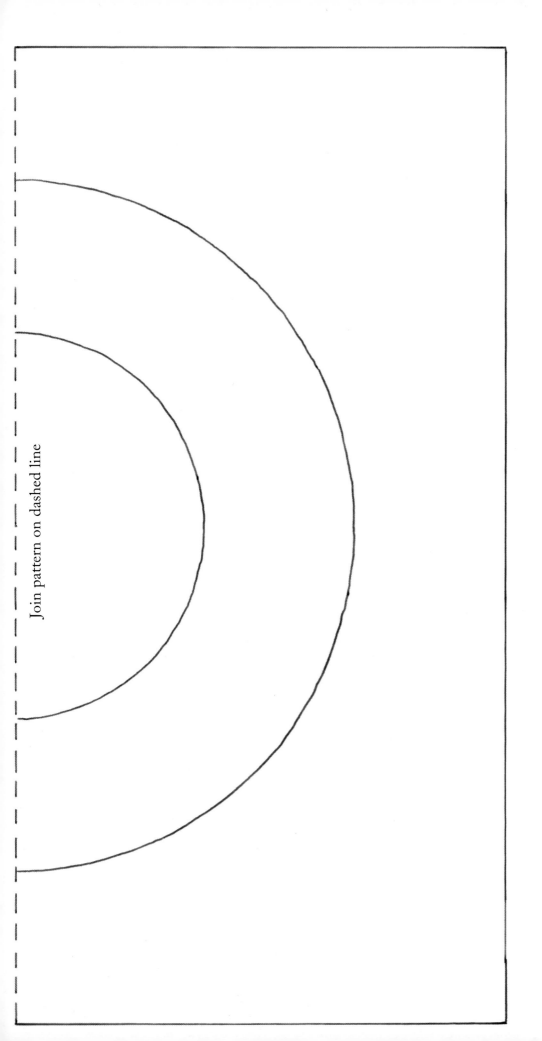

Join pattern on dashed line

43

Folk Art Pillow
(page 11)

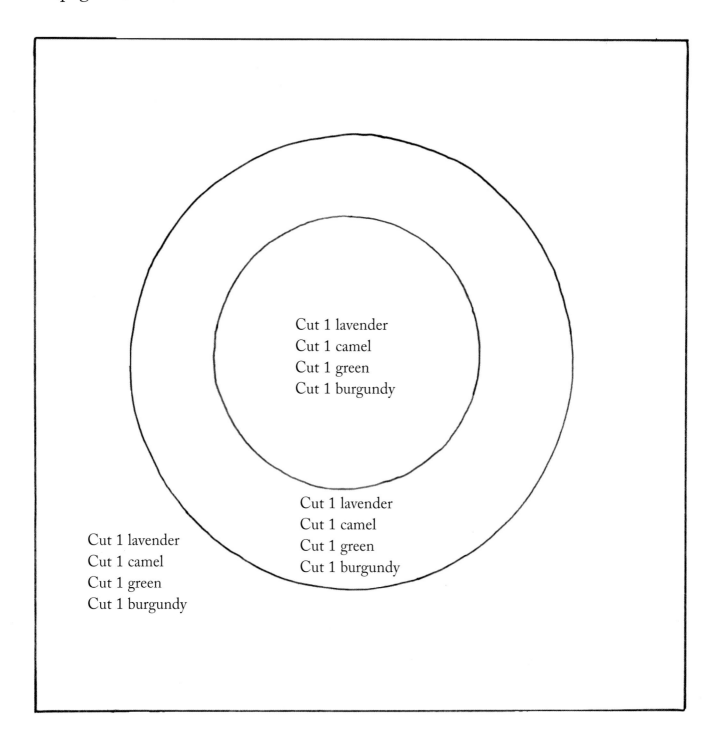

Cut 1 lavender
Cut 1 camel
Cut 1 green
Cut 1 burgundy

Cut 1 lavender
Cut 1 camel
Cut 1 green
Cut 1 burgundy

Cut 1 lavender
Cut 1 camel
Cut 1 green
Cut 1 burgundy

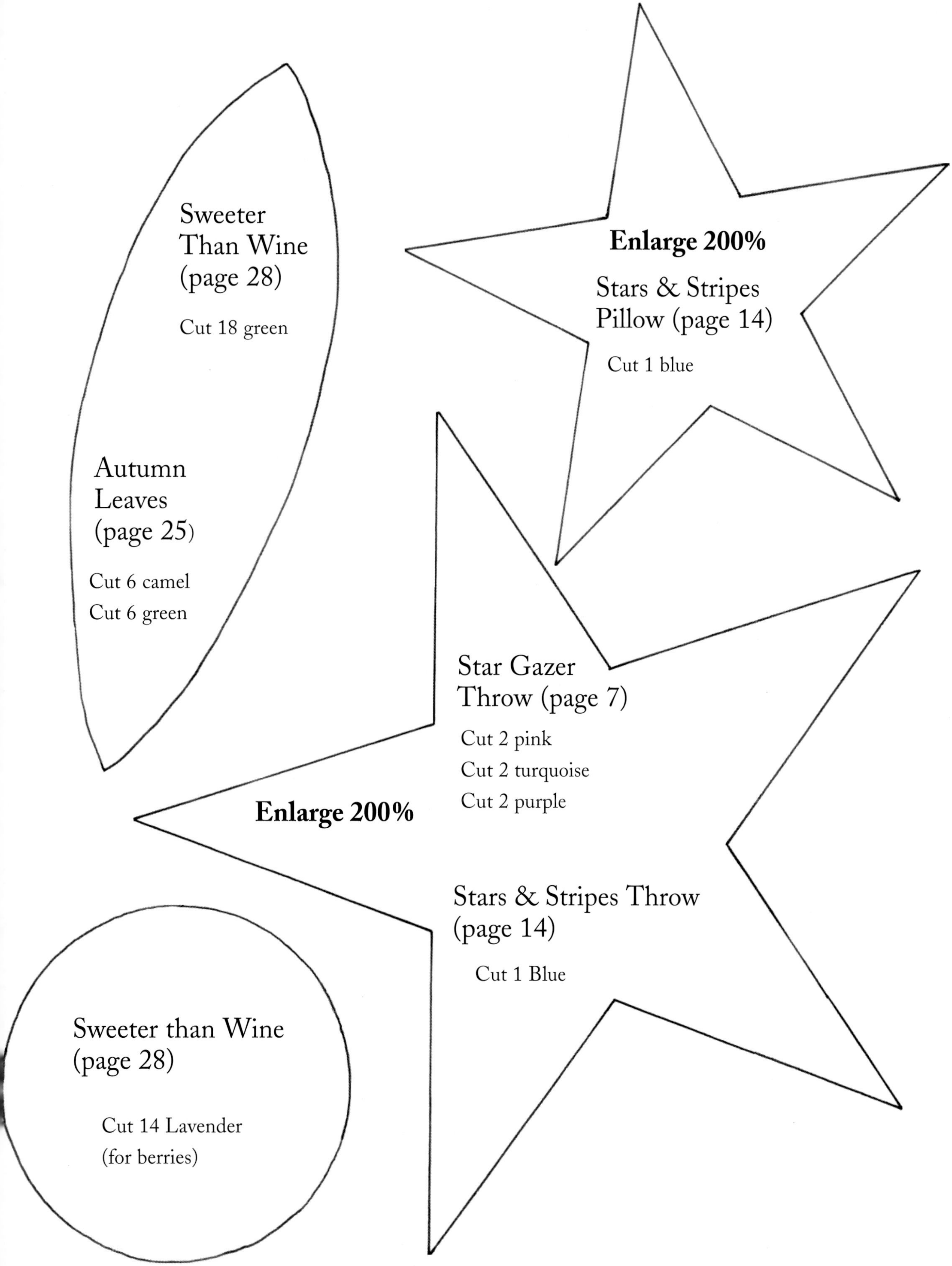

Sweeter
Than Wine
(page 28)

Cut 18 green

Enlarge 200%

Stars & Stripes
Pillow (page 14)

Cut 1 blue

Autumn
Leaves
(page 25)

Cut 6 camel
Cut 6 green

Star Gazer
Throw (page 7)

Cut 2 pink
Cut 2 turquoise
Cut 2 purple

Enlarge 200%

Stars & Stripes Throw
(page 14)

Cut 1 Blue

Sweeter than Wine
(page 28)

Cut 14 Lavender
(for berries)

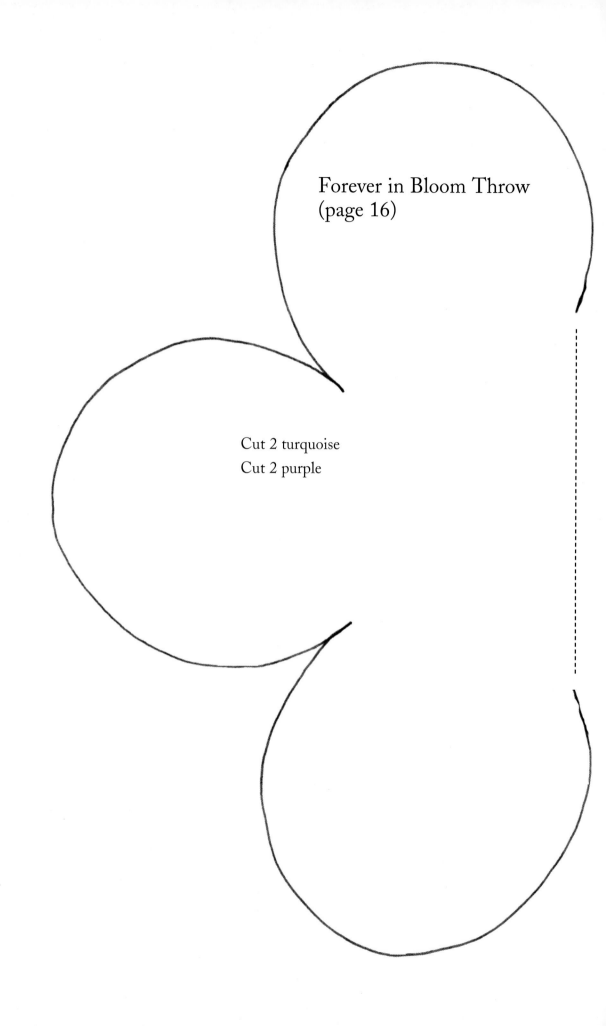

Forever in Bloom Throw
(page 16)

Cut 2 turquoise
Cut 2 purple

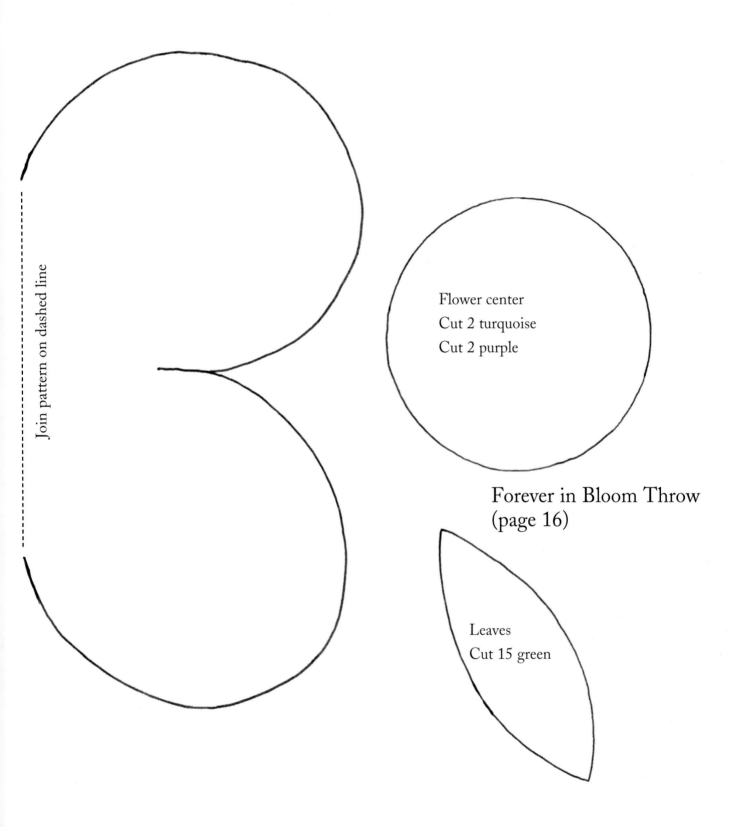

Join pattern on dashed line

Flower center
Cut 2 turquoise
Cut 2 purple

Forever in Bloom Throw
(page 16)

Leaves
Cut 15 green

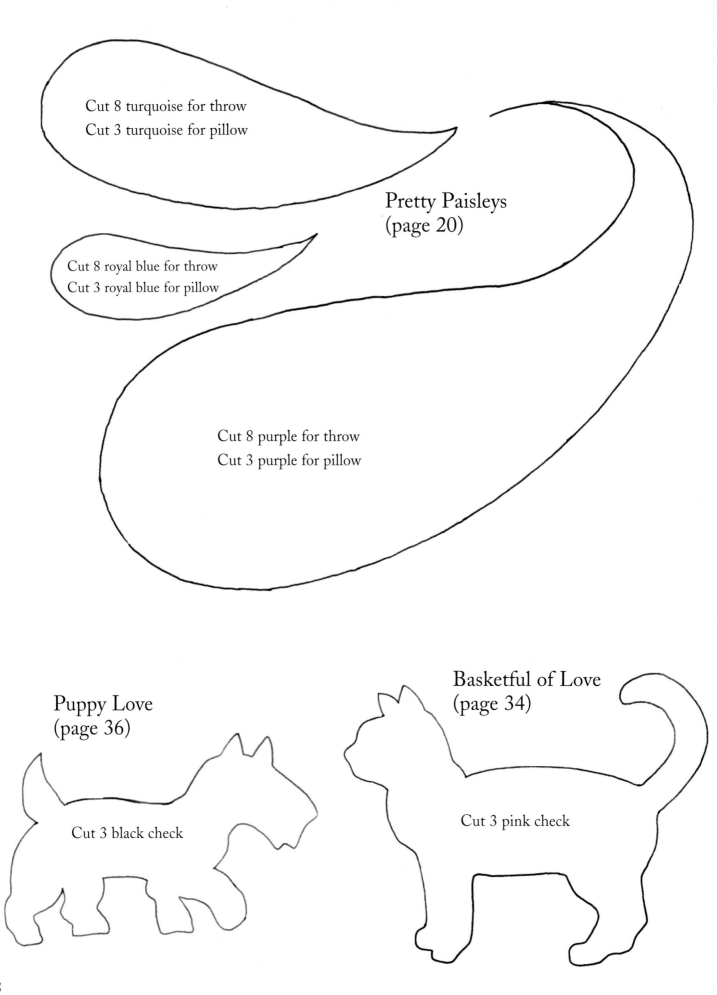

Cut 8 turquoise for throw
Cut 3 turquoise for pillow

Pretty Paisleys
(page 20)

Cut 8 royal blue for throw
Cut 3 royal blue for pillow

Cut 8 purple for throw
Cut 3 purple for pillow

Puppy Love
(page 36)

Basketful of Love
(page 34)

Cut 3 black check

Cut 3 pink check